Learning to Write
Pronouns

WEIGL PUBLISHERS INC.

Published by Weigl Publishers Inc.
350 5th Avenue, Suite 3304, PMB 6G
New York, NY 10118-0069

Website: www.weigl.com
Copyright ©2010 WEIGL PUBLISHERS INC.

All of the Internet URLs given in the book were valid at the time of publication. However, due to the
dynamic nature of the Internet, some addresses may have changed, or sites may have ceased to exist
since publication. While the author and publisher regret any inconvenience this may cause readers,
no responsibility for any such changes can be accepted by either the author or the publisher.

Library of Congress Cataloging-in-Publication Data

Lambert, Deborah.
 Pronouns / Deborah Lambert.
    p. cm. -- (Learning to write)
 Includes webliography and index.
 ISBN 978-1-60596-043-2 (hard cover : alk. paper) -- ISBN 978-1-60596-619-9 (soft cover : alk.
paper)
 1. English language--Pronoun--Juvenile literature. I. Title.
 PE1261.L36 2009
 425--dc22
                                    2009001948

Printed in China
1 2 3 4 5 6 7 8 9 0 13 12 11 10 09

Editor: Deborah G. Lambert
Design: Terry Paulhus

Photograph Credits

Weigl acknowledges Getty images as its image supplier for this title.

All of the internet URLs given in the book were valid at the time of publication. However, due to the
dynamic nature of the internet, some addresses may have changed, or sites may have ceased to exist
since publication. While the author and publisher regret any inconvenience this may cause readers,
no responsibility for any such changes can be accepted by either the author or the publisher.

Every reasonable effort has been made to trace ownership and to obtain permission to reprint
copyright material. The publishers would be pleased to have any errors or omissions brought
to their attention so that they may be corrected in subsequent printings.

Table of Contents

What is a Pronoun?

A pronoun is a part of speech that takes the place of a **noun**. It can also point to or identify a noun. A pronoun helps to avoid repeating the same noun too often. Some examples of pronouns include *I, me, him, her, she, it, they, this, them, these,* and *those*.

Some pronouns have been used to point to or take the place of their nouns in these paragraphs about Thanksgiving Day. They are shaded red.

Thanksgiving Day is a national holiday held on the fourth Thursday of November. It was first celebrated more than 370 years ago by the **pilgrims** *and the* **Wampanoag Native Americans**.

Today, Americans celebrate Thanksgiving Day with family and friends. They enjoy a large afternoon meal. This often includes corn, sweet potatoes, cranberries, and pumpkin pie. The main dish is usually a big, stuffed turkey.

In the second sentence, instead of repeating the noun "Thanksgiving Day," the pronoun "it" is used. In the fourth sentence, the pronoun "they" is used to replace the noun "Americans." Can you tell which pronoun has been used to identify or point to the noun "meal"?

Finding the Pronouns

Some pronouns have been used in this story describing the first Thanksgiving. Find the pronouns, and make a list of them in your notebook.

In 1620, a group of pilgrims sailed from Europe to the United States. They came on a ship called the Mayflower. The pilgrims settled in Plymouth, Massachusetts. They first arrived in Plymouth during the winter. The pilgrims had very little food to eat. Almost half of them died.

Two Wampanoag American Indians named Squanto and Samoset helped the pilgrims. They showed them how to farm the land and build their homes.

By the next autumn, the pilgrims had food to eat and homes to live in. They celebrated this with a harvest festival. The Wampanoag were invited to eat with them. The celebration, now called Thanksgiving, lasted for three days.

Read the Plymouth Thanksgiving story at **www.2020tech.com/thanks/ temp.html#story**. Look for other pronouns on this website, and add them to your list.

Identifying Types of Pronouns

There are many types of pronouns. These include personal, indefinite, and those that point to or identify nouns.

Personal pronouns stand for specific people, places, or things. Some include *I, me, you, he, him, she, her, it, we, us, they,* and *them.*

Indefinite pronouns replace nouns without specifying what or who the nouns are. Some include *everyone, someone, everybody, somebody, everything, something, everywhere, somewhere, each, all, most, others,* and *some.*

Pronouns that point to nouns include *this, that, these,* and *those.* They are used to identify specific nouns.

Examples of some types of pronouns are shaded red in this paragraph about Presidents' Day. Presidents' Day is a national holiday celebrated in the United States on the third Monday in February.

As citizens of the United States, everybody shows appreciation for all our presidents on Presidents' Day. This is a patriotic holiday. It is a day to honor our presidents for the roles they have played in the success of the United States.

In the paragraph, the pronoun "they" is a personal pronoun. What other types of pronouns do you see in this paragraph?

Selecting Types of Pronouns

Find the pronouns used in these paragraphs about George Washington, and list them in your notebook. Then, next to each one, name the type of pronoun it is.

*In 1789, George Washington was voted the first president of the United States. He is often called the "father of the Country." He left us, the American citizens, a **legacy** of freedom from British rule. For more than 200 years, we, as citizens, have celebrated George Washington's birthday. It became a national holiday in 1885. In 1932, festivities were held everywhere, throughout the year to mark the two hundredth anniversary of George Washington's birth. This was done to honor him.*

*The citizens of Laredo, Texas, have celebrated the **anniversary** of Washington's birthday since 1898. The events last about two weeks. Some include the Birthnight Ball, fireworks, music, and parades.*

Visit **www.kidzworld.com/article/399-presidents-day** to read more about Presidents' Day. Look for the different types of pronouns on this website, and add them to your list.

Learning about Personal Pronouns

Personal pronouns replace nouns that refer to specific people, places, or things. They can be either singular or plural.

Singular personal pronouns talk about "one" person, place, or thing. They include *I, me, you, he, him, she, her,* and *it.* Plural pronouns talk about "more than one" person, place, or thing. Plural personal pronouns include *we, us, you, they,* and *them.*

In this paragraph about Christopher Columbus, some of the personal pronouns have been shaded red.

Christopher Columbus was born in Genoa, Italy in 1451. At the age of 14, he began a seafaring career. For years, Columbus asked the leaders of many European countries to help him pay for the voyage he wanted to make around the world. They refused to help him. In 1492, Columbus talked to King Ferdinand and Queen Isabella I of Spain. They gave him money for his voyage.

In the paragraph, "he" is the personal pronoun that takes the place of a specific person, Christopher Columbus. Make a list of the other personal pronouns in the paragraph. Then, next to each pronoun, write down the noun it replaces. Which of these pronouns are singular? Which of these are plural?

Identifying Personal Pronouns

Read these paragraphs about Dr. Martin Luther King, Jr. carefully. Find the personal pronouns, and make a list of these pronouns in your notebook. Then, next to each pronoun, write down the noun it replaces. Which of these pronouns are singular? Which of these are plural?

*On Martin Luther King, Jr. Day, we honor the life of Dr Martin Luther King, Jr. He worked very hard to make sure that we could all be free. He believed that all of us should stand up for our **civil rights**. He knew that the best way to do this was through love, not violence.*

*Today, thousands of people march in parades to show they are grateful for Dr. King's efforts. To celebrate, some attend special church services. Others go to **conferences** and listen to their leaders talk about peace and civil rights.*

Visit **www.americanrhetoric.com/speeches/mlkihaveadream.htm** to read Martin Luther King, Jr.'s well-known speech, *I Have a Dream*. Look for more personal pronouns in his speech, and add them to your list.

Learning about Indefinite Pronouns

Indefinite pronouns refer to people or things without specifying who or what they are. They can be either singular or plural.

Indefinite pronouns that end in "one" are always singular. These include words, such as *anyone, everyone, one,* and *someone.* Those that end in "body" or "thing" are always singular. They include words, such as *anybody, somebody, everybody, nobody, anything, something,* and *everything.*

The indefinite pronouns *many, others, few,* and *several* are always plural. *All, most, some, more, any,* and *none* can be singular or plural depending on how they are used.

In this paragraph about the celebration of Cinco de Mayo, indefinite pronouns are used. They are shaded red. Cinco de Mayo, which means "the fifth of May," is celebrated across Mexico and the United States every year on that date.

To celebrate Cinco de Mayo, crowds of people gather in the streets to hear lively music. Some, including children, join in the parades. Others watch colorful dance shows. Everyone eats the tasty food made just for the events.

Make a list of the pronouns shaded in the paragraph in your notebook. Then, next to each one, write down whether it is singular or plural.

To learn more about Cinco de Mayo, visit **www.kiddyhouse.com/ Holidays/Cinco**. Look for examples of indefinite pronouns on this website, and add them to your list.

Identifying Indefinite Pronouns

Read these paragraphs about the history of Passover carefully. Find the indefinite pronouns, and make a list of these pronouns in your notebook. Then, draw a chart like the one on this page, and place the pronouns in their correct columns. One has been done for you.

*In ancient Egypt, the Pharaoh, or ruler, kept the **Hebrews** as slaves. The Hebrews wanted to be free. They prayed to their God for help. Everyone kept hoping that God would help them. Then, someone came to their rescue. A young prince named Moses asked the Pharaoh to free them.*

The Pharaoh refused, and so ten plagues were sent to Egypt. One of the plagues was the death of the firstborn sons of anyone who did not have a mark made with the blood of a lamb on their doors.

The Hebrews believed that their God had told Moses to have them make a mark with the blood of a lamb on their doors so that the Angel of Death would "pass over" them. Therefore, they all had the mark on their doors. Their sons were saved. The Egyptians did not believe that anything would happen to their sons. None of them had the mark on their doors. Their firstborn sons died.

INDEFINITE PRONOUNS	
Singular	**Plural**
Everyone	all

Learning about Pronouns that Point to Nouns

Pronouns that point to nouns identify and specify those nouns. *This* and *these* refer to nouns that are nearby in time or space. *That* or *those* refer to nouns that are farther away in time or space. *This* and *that* refer to singular nouns. *Those* and *these* refer to plural nouns.

In these sentences about the history of **Veterans** Day, some pronouns that point to nouns have been used. Which nouns do these pronouns point to?

On Veterans Day, Americans honor those who served in all wars.

Armed forces fought in trenches. These were forts dug into the ground.

*To end World War I, the Armistice Treaty was signed. That was a peace agreement between Germany and the **Allied Powers**.*

Veterans Day is observed every year on November 11. To read more about Veterans Day, go to **www.va.gov/kids/k-5/multicontent. asp?intPageId=3**.

Identifying Pronouns that Point to Nouns

These sentences give some information about events that led to and take place on Veterans Day. Find the pronouns that point to nouns. Then, next to each pronoun, write down the noun to which it points.

In San Francisco, California, many people visited the Moving Wall. *This is a traveling wall that contains engraved names of American soldiers who lost their lives in the Vietnam War. It is half the size of the war memorial in Washington, DC.*

On the Vietnam Veterans Memorial Wall, there are 58,249 names of those who died and those who remain missing from the Vietnam War.

At 11:00 A.M. on Veterans Day, Americans stop what they are doing for two minutes. They pay their respect to wartime and peacetime heroes. This is a Veterans Day **tradition**.

President Woodrow Wilson outlined his goals to end the war. He created an organization that promoted international cooperation. The organization called the League of Nations was created in 1919.

Where Do They Belong?

In learning to use pronouns, you should be able to identify the different types when they are used. Pronouns have been used in these paragraphs about the history of Memorial Day. Some of the pronouns are shaded red. On Memorial Day, veterans, military personnel, and citizens pay tribute to servicemen and women.

Memorial Day was first called "Decoration Day." It was named for the practice of "decorating" graves with flowers to remember those who died serving the country.

In October, 1864, Emma Hunter, Sophie Keller, and Elizabeth Meyers began decorating soldiers' graves in Pennsylvania. A year later, everyone gathered to help them decorate the graves. Today, a sign outside Boalsburg, Pennsylvania, reads: "Birthplace of Memorial Day."

In these paragraphs, examples of personal pronouns include "it" and "They." "It" is singular, and "they" is plural. "Those" is an example of a pronoun that points to a noun.

Make a list of the other pronouns in the paragaph. What types of pronouns are they?

Grouping Pronouns

In these sentences about Cinco de Mayo, different types of pronouns are used. Find all of the pronouns, and in your notebook, place them in a chart like the one on this page. Three examples have been done for you.

On Cinco de Mayo, everyone who celebrates eats special foods, such as **gorditas** *and* **buñuelos.**

Cinco de Mayo celebrations include carnivals, fairs, games, parades, and fireworks. These are exciting ways to celebrate being Mexican.

One of the most exciting events on Cinco de Mayo takes place after dark. This is a colorful display of fireworks that light up the night sky.

Los Angeles, California, has the largest Cinco de Mayo celebration in the country. Thousands of people attend this celebration. Some play games and buy crafts, while others watch the colorful parades.

In Minnesota, we Mexicans and Mexican Americans attend St. Paul's Cinco de Mayo celebration. Visitors enjoy a parade, dancing, music, food, and even a car show with us.

PRONOUNS		
Personal	**Indefinite**	**Point to Nouns**
we	Some	This

Using Pronouns to Create Sentences

Like nouns, pronouns are important parts of a sentence, paragraph, or story. Imagine trying to write sentences without using pronouns.

Read these sentences about the celebration of Independence Day on the Fourth of July. No pronouns have been used in these sentences.

After the Declaration of Independence was adopted, the Declaration of Independence was distributed to the public.

On Independence Day, Americans do not have to work, so Americans have time to spend with their families.

In the first sentence, the noun "Declaration of Independence" has been repeated. To avoid repeating that noun, the personal pronoun "it" can be used. When this pronoun is used, the sentence will read like this.

> After the Declaration of Independence was adopted, it was distributed to the public.

Which pronoun could replace the noun "Americans" in the second sentence?

Creating Your Own Sentences Using Types of Pronouns

In these sentences about Independence Day and its history, no pronouns have been used. Study the sentences carefully. Then, rewrite them using the correct pronouns to replace, refer, or point to the nouns used.

On Independence Day, Americans wanted to honor the day Americans gained their independence.

*On Independence Day, people wave American flags as marching bands and beautiful **floats** pass people by.*

*King George III did not want to give up control over the colonies, so King George III sent soldiers to the colonies to control any **rebellion** that might take place.*

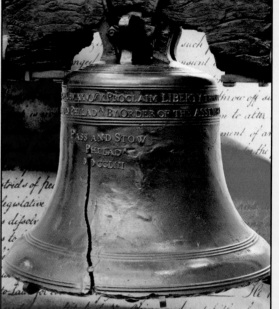

The Liberty Bell was hung in the Philadelphia State House tower in 1753, and on July 8, 1776, the Liberty Bell rang to celebrate the adoption of the Declaration of Independence.

There are symbols that help remind Americans of their freedom. The symbols include the American Flag, the Liberty Bell, and the Statue of Liberty.

To learn more about Independence Day, go to **www.just4kidsmagazine.com/ beacon4god/july4.html**.

Tools for Learning about Pronouns

What did you learn? Look at the topics in the "Skills" column. Compare them to the page number in the "Page" column. Review the content you learned about pronouns by reading the "Content" column below.

SKILLS	CONTENT	PAGE
Defining a pronoun	Thanksgiving Day celebrations, history of Thanksgiving Day	4–5
Identifying types of pronouns	Presidents' Day, George Washington	6–7
Learning about personal pronouns	Christopher Columbus, Dr. Martin Luther King Jr.	8–9
Learning about indefinite pronouns	Cinco de Mayo celebrations, history of Passover	10–11
Learning about pronouns that point to nouns	History of Veterans Day, celebration of Veterans Day	12–13
Grouping pronouns according to type	History of Memorial Day, Cinco de Mayo celebrations	14–15
Using pronouns	Independence Day celebrations	16–17

Practice Writing Your Own Paragraphs
Using Different Types of Pronouns

During holiday celebrations, Americans often play different games. For example, on Labor Day, some people play baseball and take part in three-legged races.

Write two paragraphs describing two games that you play with your family or friends on any two of the holidays that you celebrate. Use some of the types of pronouns explained in this book to write about these games.

The following are pictures of games played on Thanksgiving Day and Labor Day. You may choose to write about these games.

Put Your Knowledge to Use

Election Day in the United States of America is the Tuesday following the first Monday in November. On this day, any of the states can hold an election. On Election Day, most Americans 18 years of age or older can vote.

On January 20, 2008, Barack Obama was sworn in as the 44th President of the United States. To read Barack Obama's inaugural address, go to **www.cnn.com/2009/POLITICS/01/20/obama.politics /index.html**.

Study the types of pronouns used in his speech. Make a list of all the pronouns, and the nouns that they pointed to or replaced. Imagine you have been elected president. Use some of these pronouns to write your own inaugural address.

President Barack Obama gave his inaugural address in Washington, DC, on January 20, 2009.

Use the Internet, or visit the library to find more information about another national holiday celebrated in the United States, not mentioned in this book. Write a story describing how that day is celebrated. Use the pronouns that you learned in this book in your story.

You can start with some information about how Halloween is celebrated. The following pictures show some of the costumes children wear and how squash is designed during Halloween. You can start with these.

Other Parts of Speech

You have now learned the tools for using pronouns. You can use your knowledge of pronouns to write clear and interesting sentences, paragraphs, or stories. There are four other parts of speech. You can use some of the same tools you learned in this book to use these other parts of speech. The chart below shows the other parts of speech and their key features.

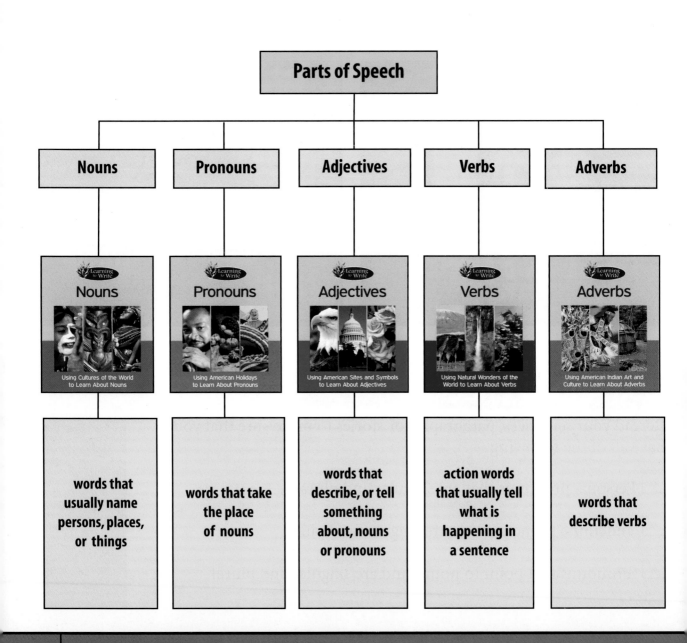

Parts of Speech

Nouns	Pronouns	Adjectives	Verbs	Adverbs
Learning to Write — Nouns — Using Cultures of the World to Learn About Nouns	*Learning to Write* — Pronouns — Using American Holidays to Learn About Pronouns	*Learning to Write* — Adjectives — Using American Sites and Symbols to Learn About Adjectives	*Learning to Write* — Verbs — Using Natural Wonders of the World to Learn About Verbs	*Learning to Write* — Adverbs — Using American Indian Art and Culture to Learn About Adverbs
words that usually name persons, places, or things	words that take the place of nouns	words that describe, or tell something about, nouns or pronouns	action words that usually tell what is happening in a sentence	words that describe verbs

Further Research

Books

Many books provide information on pronouns. To learn more about how to use different types of pronouns, you can borrow books from the library. To learn more about American holidays, try reading these books.

Balfour, Barbara. *Thanksgiving Day*. New York, NY: Weigl Publishers Inc., 2007.

Foran, Jill. *Independence Day*. New York, NY: Weigl Publishers Inc., 2004.

Foran, Jill. *Martin Luther King Jr. Day*. New York, NY: Weigl Publishers Inc., 2004.

Websites

On the Internet, you can type terms, such as "pronouns" or "types of pronouns," into the search bar of your Web browser, and click the search button. It will take you to a number of sites with this information.

Read more about American holidays at **www.history.com/genericContent.do?id=53343** and **www.ringsurf.com/online/1757-american_holidays.html**.

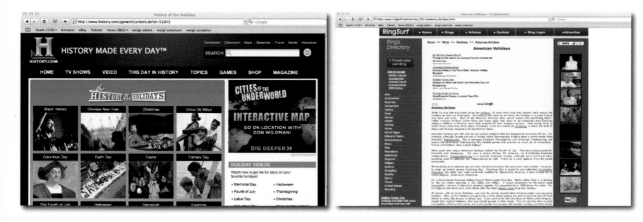

Glossary

Allied Powers: a military partnership between 28 countries that are in opposition to another group of countries during World War I

anniversary: the date on which an event took place in a previous year

buñuelos: deep-fried pastries that are similar to doughnuts

civil rights: the political and social struggle for racial equality for African Americans

conferences: meetings

floats: low, flat platforms on wheels in parades

gorditas: thick tortillas stuffed with meat, vegetables, or cheese

Hebrews: another name for the Jewish people and their language

legacy: a thing handed down by a person who held a job or office before the current holder

noun: the part of speech that is usually used to name a person, place, or thing

pilgrims: British travelers who journeyed to the United States in 1620

rebellion: resistance or fight against a government, ruler, or tradition

tradition: a custom or way of doing something every year

veterans: people who have served in the armed forces

Wampanoag American Indians: American Indians who lived in Massachusettes long before the pilgrims arrived

Index